pencil on paper, always and forever more

Christina Brooke Faulk

BookLeaf Publishing

India | USA | UK

Presentation by *BookLeaf Publishing*

Web: www.bookleafpub.com

E-mail: info@bookleafpub.com

ISBN: 9789358316735

First edition 2023

"I was always able to write my way out"

-Florence + the Machine

for the pencil on paper that never left me

for the heartaches that have yet to heal

for every person who inspired these words

for who I've been, for who I am,

for who I will be

and above all,

to every person who asked for this

thank you for giving me the courage. <3

I Wrote a Book About You

I wrote a book about you.
But not the kind that anyone can read.
It's a novel of stories, made up in my head
About the person I thought you'd be.
Intelligent, warm, respectful, kind.
A loving heart, a gentle touch,
A smile that doesn't fade in time.
Of course they were just stories,
Sweet, fictitious illusions.
What a pretty picture was painted.
I can't help but wonder, who was the artist?
Perhaps it was I with a brush in hand,
Painting a colorful portrait of the
Mask you wore.
An image you created.
I suppose we each had a rendition.
Oddly similar in the same way
Fairy tales reflect the Brothers Grimm.
Whereas one has happy endings,
The other is gruesome and murderous.
Somehow though, it's the same story.

I wrote a book about you.
It's a novel of stories, made up in my head.

Gravity

One look at you and I caught a glimpse
of what my future could be.
But it was only a glimpse.
A blink of an eye.
You were gravity.
Like Mother Earth keeps her moon
just close enough.
You pulled me in
just close enough to touch.
And far enough away
to know I could not stay.
But much like the Moon affects the Earth's oceans,
I at least once touched on your emotions.
A mere moment in time,
short, sweet, everlasting.
The magic between us, spellcasting.
You were gravity.
And I,
I was but a helpless moon.

Another

Another "forever," another lie
Another "goodbye," I don't want to cry.
Another heartbreak, another mistake,
Another "baby, this is all I can take."
Another boy, another tear.
Another lonely night, another fear.
Another dream, another nightmare
Another one gone, another "take care."
Another hope, another light
Another word, another fight.
Another morning, another day
Another path, another way.
Another girl, another face
Another town, another place.
Another lyric, another song
Another one that won't last long.
Another look, another life.
Another heart, another strife.
Another question, another "why?"
Another "forever," another lie.

Cynthia

Here I am spinning circles with you again
You come in like a storm that won't seem to end.
You're reckless and wild, careless, insane
You're chaotic and messy, my own hurricane.
You sabotage me when you come around
When you finally leave, I'm again on the ground
Picking up pieces, cleaning up your mess
Without you my life doesn't have all this stress.
So I send you away again, time after time
And then for a while I start to feel fine.
Somehow though, you always find your way back
And it again feels like I'm under attack
I can't seem to escape you and I don't know why
Though sometimes I feel like I don't even try.
Each time you come back it's seemingly worse
And I can't keep on living with you and your curse.
I don't want to say goodbye to you forever
But it seems like I have to if I want to get better.
You were gone for a while and my life was so good,
However, I missed you more than I should.
You have so many parts that I love and I hate,
But you're so bad for me there should be no debate.
You steal all my light with the darkness you bring,
Unfortunately, darkness is oddly comforting.
At this point it's simply a battle of will.
I have to stop spinning, I have to be still.

Never Meant To

I never meant to burden you, never meant to hurt you
Never meant to know you, never meant to show you
Never meant to want you, never meant to haunt you
Never meant to fight you, never meant to spite you
Never meant to kiss you, never meant to miss you
Never meant to touch you, never meant to love you
BUT I DID.
I burdened you with my whole heart,
and I hurt you when I fell apart.
I knew you when you didn't want to be known,
and I showed you things not meant to be shown.
I wanted you when you couldn't be kept,
and I haunted you every time that I wept.
I fought with you more times than I should
and I spited you just because I could.
I kissed you with passion and grace,
and then I missed you being in my space.
I touched you with each of my fingers,
and I loved you with a love that still lingers.

Wildfire

Looking back at us, we were the real deal.
Nothing could fabricate the way I still feel.
The moment we met, with your sweet shy smile,
Who knew we'd become something so vile?!
Right person, wrong place, wrong time in my life.
I wasn't quite ready to become your wife.
You roped me and reined me, put me in a fence.
My wild heart couldn't take it, it didn't make sense.
I loved you truly, as much as I could.
But you didn't love me how I thought you should.
I was a wildfire, a force uncontrolled.
You couldn't take it, let the story be told.
Some days you were gas, igniting the flames.
Others you were water, but I couldn't be tamed.
Another time, another place, we may have worked out.
I was too young to know what real love is about.
We both tried so hard, we gave it our all.
Perhaps in the next life we won't have to fall.

A Moment

There are select few moments in life
which forever change the course of fate.
Perhaps a moment which never should have occurred,
while also a moment where you'd forever return.
Perhaps a moment you'd take back given the chance,
while also a moment that made your heart dance.
Perhaps a moment that would destroy your soul,
while also a moment you felt you struck gold.
Perhaps a moment that would steal your light,
while also a moment that you couldn't fight.
Perhaps a moment riddled with deceit,
while also a moment your soul felt peace.
Perhaps a moment that never was real,
while also a moment that you can still feel.
The sun on your face, grass between your toes;
Brown eyes turned gold with the sunset
as the calm breeze blows.
There are select few moments in life
which forever change the course of fate.

A Decade Later

Ten years ago I ran from you,
Ten years ago you met her.
Ten years ago I "found" myself,
Ten years ago you met her.
Ten years ago I was so free,
Ten years ago you met her.
Ten years ago you may've loved me
But ten years ago you met her.
Ten years have passed
since I saw you last
and somehow I still love you.
A gentle love, a peaceful love,
a distant love for you.
Your life with her is beautiful,
I'd want nothing less for you.

Forever Running

I never was one to keep relationships alive.
Not even just those of the romantic kind.
I never was close with cousins, nor had many friends.
I've never understood why everything ends.
But I never felt lonely when I was young and free.
Life was a joyride, happiness came easily.
I lived a life with no boundaries, always on the run.
You could tell me nothing, I was just having fun.
Somewhere on my journey, I caught up with myself.
All those years of running took their toll on my health.
I littered this country with pieces of my heart and soul,
Then I looked in the mirror to see I'd lost control.
Mistakes and regrets, no doubt I have plenty.
And I can't recall when I started feeling so empty.
Is a life on the run one worth living at all?
When nowadays I just stumble and fall.
But I keep standing up, I try to stay stable.
Although I'm alone, I know that I am able.
I'll get through this madness, though no easy feat.
I know that this sadness can indeed be beat.
I'll do it myself, as I always have done.
But I'll never forfeit this life on the run.

I Love You

I always dreamed of a love so true,
always had an aching for romance.
I always believed it would happen for me,
so I latched on whenever I got the chance.
Say my name? I love you. Hold my hand? I love you.
Let's take a trip? I love you. Touch my body? I love you.
Sing a song? I love you. Look in my eyes? I love you.
Drive all night? I love you. Sit by the water? I love you.
Spin me around? I love you. Pull me in? I love you.
Push me away? I love you. Ignore me all day? I love you.
Scream in my face? I love you. Tell a bold face lie? I love you.
Push me to the ground? I love you. Steal my light? I love you.
Leave without goodbye? I love you. Did you make me cry?
I love you. I love you. I love you.
I always dreamed of a love so true,
it's such a shame that I believed true love was you.

Romeo

You were my very first dream come true.
I'd never gotten what I wanted, until I wanted you.
The love your brown eyes had for me,
I can still feel it, when I try hard enough.
Never again have I felt that kind of love.
It took so many years for me to know
what it was that I lost when I let you go.
I had all but forgotten the way you make me feel,
A decade has passed, but the love is still real.
It's different now than it was then, it's grown.
A love for a man who I'd never have known.
Not a romantic, jealous, passionate love,
but a respectful, warm, understanding love.
More than loving a memory, more than loving a man.
I love you deeply, purely, compassionately.
I told you many times that I'd love you forever,
only now have I learned what forever means.

I Wish

I wish that we could go back to the way it was before
when you and I could banter and there was nothing more.
I wish that I could take away everything I said
about how much I hate you and I wish that I was dead.
I wish I could forget the moment I first saw your smile
and how it was the kindest one I'd seen in quite a while.
I wish you'd never touched me when I asked you not to.
Not that I didn't want it, I just knew what it would do.
I wish you never spoke my name with that look in your eye.
The thought of that to this day still makes me want to cry.
I wish you weren't so far away, I miss you all the time.
Not that it matters anyhow, it was a perfect crime.
I wish I didn't feel this way, I wish I didn't care.
The moment that your eyes met mine, we were so unaware.
I wish it wasn't ending, I'm so afraid to go.
I do not want to lose this, for I will miss you so.
I wish that we could go back to the way it was before.
But we're past the point of no return, it hurts me to my core.

Blame

I can't be mad at anyone but me
for all of the things that I let be.
I can't blame you for being who you are,
and I can't blame you for taking it too far.
I can't blame you for taking parts of my soul,
and I can't blame you for losing all control.
I can't blame you for how I feel,
and I can't blame you for not being real.
I can't blame you for good advice,
and I can't blame you for paying the price.
I can't blame you for things going south,
and I can't blame you for my running mouth.
I can't blame you for what occurred,
and I can't blame you for loving her.
I can only blame myself for my own faults.
This rambling mind and these wild thoughts.
I can't be mad at anyone but me.
I can't be mad, because now I can see.

Blessed

How blessed I once was
to have never known your face
to have never felt your touch
to have never tasted your lips
to have never been destroyed by you
But oh, my darling,
if not for that then I couldn't understand
how blessed I am in knowing
that I will never see you again

Only In My Dreams

If we could be together, but only in my dreams,
then I would sleep forever, and we could sew our seams.
If you and I could run away,
and watch this world turn 'round,
then let us not waste today,
let's leave without a sound.
If by chance, we meet again,
and your lips fall upon mine,
then to your hands my heart I'd send
until the end of time.

To The One

To the one I loved first,
I don't think I would have known
how to love if not for you.
Then again, maybe I would have.

To the one I loved next,
you put up with me for the longest.
I will forever respect you for that.
I wish we could find a way
to be friends.

To the one I loved next,
you didn't mean to hurt me.
I forgive you for doing so.

To the one I loved next,
I'm sorry for running away.
You deserved more.
I'm so happy that you got it.

To the one I loved next,
I hope you are the last.
You lit a fire within me,
and our life together went up in flames.
I didn't mean to burn you.

Of all the love I've shared,
each with their own meaning,
I just hope, with all of me,
one day I will love myself.

By the Lake

"I remember the woman by the lake on the rocks."
Unfortunately that sweet woman got lost.
She was so peaceful, content, light, and kind.
But somewhere along the way she lost her poor mind.
Years spent alone in the house on the hill,
She simmered in anger and lost her free will.
The sadness she married brought such darkness in.
At some point in the madness she could no longer win.
Spirals and downfalls and grief, they all struck.
She tried for a while, but then she gave up.
Her body and mind, they lost all control.
But somewhere inside she still has her soul.
That woman from then took so long to find.
I'll find her again, I just have to try.
I won't find her for you, I have to find her for me.
Though I do hope in time you'll be able to see;
That woman you met by the lake on the rocks,
She's not gone forever, right now she's just lost.

Rock Bottom

How far down is rock bottom?
I feel like I've been crawling on the floor of the sea
When I feel I've reached it,
It falls out from beneath me.
How far down is rock bottom?
I feel like I've been there before
When I feel I'll start to stand,
I get knocked back down on the floor.
How far down is rock bottom?
I feel like I've been living here forever
When I feel like I've escaped,
I quickly learn I'm still not better.
How far down is rock bottom?
I feel like I must have gotten there by now
When I feel like giving in,
I pull myself up somehow
How far down is rock bottom?
I feel like I should probably know
When I feel like I've found out,
I understand I have to heal and grow.
How far down is rock bottom?

Remember

I see you in so many dreams
And I always wonder what it might mean
It's you and me, frollicking on the beach
We're hand in hand, and we both have a drink
The waves are crashing like thunder
And you're watching as they pull me under
We're talking and laughing, and living life
Then sunset turns into a beautiful night
Now we're singing and dancing around in the bar
Those were the best times of my life, by far
I miss you often, I truly miss my friend
But I understand why we had to end
We were something rare, we had so much fun
All the way til the end, we gave it a run
I hope that you're happy, I hope we'll both be free
And I hope that you always remember me
For better and worse, both happy and sad
But above all, remember the love that we had

On A Cloud

The thunder was booming, the lightning was flashing.
The clouds were rolling in, the waves were crashing.
The wind was picking up, the rain was pouring down.
You could feel it in the air, there was fury all around.
Everything was cold, dark, frightening.
All cold rain, dark clouds, except for the lightning.
And it seemed like the storm never would end;
This storm made days and nights seem to blend.
Until one day I saw, peaking over a cloud, a golden ray.
A ray of sunshine, a light of hope for a new day.
Slowly, the sun crept out to show that perfect light.
At that moment nothing mattered, all was right.
What could be better? A rainbow, no less.
A perfect little rainbow, relieving all the stress.
A perfect rainbow with perfect clouds on each side.
It was on one of those clouds that I chose to ride.
And here I am now, laying on my cloud.
And all is at peace, and the world isn't too loud.
My spirit is rising, my heart is flying.
The knots in my stomach are finally untying.
Just laying on my cloud at the bottom of my rainbow,
Waiting for a better day that's soon to come, I just know.

www.ingramcontent.com/pod-product-compliance
Lightning Source LLC
La Vergne TN
LVHW050849200726
843508LV00013B/3000